PEOPLE THROUGH HISTORY

PEOPLE IN THE TOWN

by Karen Bryant-Mole

WAYLAND

PEOPLE THROUGH HISTORY

People in the Country
People in the Town
People at Home
People at Work
People Having Fun
People On The Move

First published in 1996 by Wayland (Publishers) Ltd.,
61 Western Road, Hove BN3 1JD, England.

© Copyright 1996 BryantMole Books
Edited by Deborah Elliott
Designed and Typeset by Chrissie Sloan
Cover design by Liz Miller

British Library Cataloguing in Publication Data
Bryant-Mole, Karen
People In The Town- (People Through History Series)
1. Title II. Series
941. 00 9732
ISBN 0 7502 1662 X

Printed and bound in Italy by G. Canale & C.S.p.A

Contents

Shopping

In the past, people used to go shopping for food every day. Now, many people only shop for food once a week or, perhaps, once a fortnight.

1910s

People did not have fridges, so they went shopping for fresh food each day. There used to be lots of small local shops like this one.

1950s

This is one of the first shopping centres. People could buy most of the things they needed from the shops in this row.

Now

Some of today's shopping centres are enormous. There are lots of different shops and cafés in one building. Shoppers can stay warm and dry.

Street traders

Street traders used to have barrows that could be pushed from place to place. Today, many street traders travel around in vans.

1890s

People bought hot coffee from this street trader's stall. The sides lifted up to form canopies. These sheltered the trader and his customers from the sun and rain.

1950s

This knife grinder pushed his barrow around the streets, asking people if they wanted their knives sharpening. He sharpened them on a spinning circle of stone.

Now

This trader drives his van around to different offices at lunchtime. Workers can buy sandwiches, drinks and baked potatoes.

Pedestrians

In the past, pedestrians often walked along roads, even in the middle of town. Today's traffic would make this a very dangerous thing to do.

1910s

These pedestrians are strolling down the main road. Few people had cars in the 1910s. Most people travelled in horse-drawn carts or carriages.

1950s

By this time there was much more traffic on the roads. The school crossing lady in the picture is helping these children to cross the road safely.

Now

There is so much traffic on the roads today that some towns have areas for pedestrians only. These are much safer than busy roads. They are cleaner and quieter, too.

Living in the town

Some people live in town houses that were built many years ago. Outside they look much the same as they did then, but inside they are very different.

1890s

Many poorer townspeople lived in homes that were crowded together in narrow streets. The houses did not have gardens, so the children played together in the streets.

1930s

Housing estates were built on the outskirts of towns. There was a lot more space and the houses had gardens where the children could play.

PRICES FROM £139,950

PRINCE of WALES COURT

3 BEDROOM
2 BATHROOM APARTMENTS
AND PENTHOUSES

SHOW APARTMENT OPEN DAILY 10AM - 4PM

Now

Today, many old town houses have been made into several smaller flats. Some people live in new, specially-built blocks of flats. Most flats have no garden. Some flats have shared gardens.

11

Garages

Many garages were once horse stables. Now, people drive there to buy oil and petrol for their cars. Some garages have workshops where cars can be checked or repaired.

1900s

People could have their horses looked after at these town centre stables. A sign says that they could also have motors cleaned and stored here.

1930s

The owner of this garage served petrol to customers. Drivers didn't have to get out of their cars at all. This owner also mended cars and motorbikes.

Now

Today, garages are self-service. This means that drivers have to fill up their petrol tanks themselves. Many garages are open all day and all night.

Eating out

Waitresses in cafés used to serve customers at their tables. Now, many cafés are self-service, where people queue up for their food and drink.

1940s

The waitresses in this café wore white aprons. They took orders from customers and then bought the tea or coffee to their tables.

1950s

Self-service cafés were becoming very popular. People walked past a counter and collected their food and drink on a tray. They paid for it at the end of the counter. It was a much quicker way to serve hungry customers.

Now

Most towns have 'fast food' restaurants. People queue up at a counter for burgers, chips or baked potatoes. They can choose to eat the food in the restaurant or take it away.

Milk deliveries

In the past, people had to buy their milk every day. Today, many people buy milk from shops or supermarkets and store it in a cold fridge.

1900s

Dairies bought milk from farmers. The milk was taken around the town in large churns. Customers brought their own containers to collect the milk.

1950s

People ordered their milk from milkmen who delivered it to their front door each morning. This milkman carried the milk on a cart pulled by a horse.

Now

Today, milkmen drive milkfloats. Fewer people have their milk delivered now because it is cheaper to buy milk from supermarkets.

Going to school

Children used to learn by repeating what the teacher said or by copying what the teacher wrote. Today, schoolwork is much more interesting.

1890s

There were lots of children in a class. The teacher stood at the front and made the children repeat sums and spellings.

1910s

The desks in this class were set out in rows. Boys and girls had to sit at separate sides of the classroom.

1950s

These children sat together in small groups. They could talk to each other and to the teacher about the activity they were working on.

Now

Today, as well as learning how to read and write, children learn to use computers. Many town schools have built wildlife areas for children to study.

Going to market

Markets are, and always have been, places where people come together to buy and sell things. A town's market is usually held on the same day each week.

1900s

Farmers walked their animals from the countryside to the towns on market day. They hoped to sell them for a good price.

1950s

People bought clothes, material, household goods and food from this huge collection of covered market stalls.

Now

At this market, some people sell china, clothes and books from stalls. Others come in their cars and sell things they no longer want. The shoppers are hoping to pick up a bargain.

Going to the library

Libraries were once rather strict places, where people were only allowed to talk in whispers. Today's libraries are friendly and welcoming.

1920s

At this time, most public libraries only kept non-fiction books. These are not story books, they are books with facts.

1940s

More people wanted to borrow books, so travelling libraries went around lending or selling books. People had to pay a fee to borrow a book.

1950s

Many public libraries had special areas for children, with story books and non-fiction books. People did not have to pay money to borrow books from public libraries.

Now

Today's libraries keep every kind of book. People can borrow CDs and tapes, too. This library has bright cushions for children to sit on while they read.

Street entertainers

In many towns, street entertainers keep shoppers amused. People sometimes give the entertainer money if they have enjoyed the performance.

1910s

Lots of street entertainers used animals in their performances. The animals were often treated very badly. Many trainers used whips to make bears perform.

1930s

This entertainer played a barrel organ. The monkey was just there to make people stop and look. It would probably have preferred to be in its own country.

Now

Today's street entertainers dance, sing, mime and juggle. They still hope that people will enjoy the performance and give them some money.

Going to the hospital

New medicines and skills have changed the way people are treated. Patients often died from illnesses that can be cured today.

1910s

The patients in this hospital were treated in huge wards. Many hospital buildings were paid for by the local people. The patients had to pay whatever they could afford.

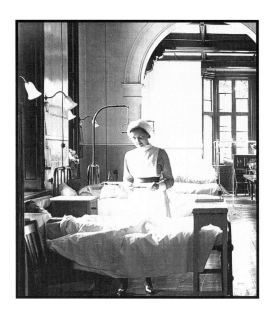

1930s

This was a public hospital, paid for by the government and by local charities. New inventions, like X-ray machines, were improving the treatment that patients were given.

1950s

Hospital treatment was free for everyone. It was part of the National Health Service which provided medical care for everyone in the country.

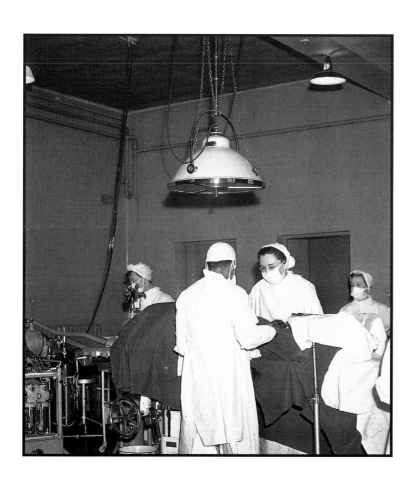

Now

Sometimes there is a long wait to see a specialist doctor or to have an operation. Some people now buy private medical insurance. They can see a doctor when and where they choose.

Going to the cinema

Before television, millions of people went to the cinema each week. Today, many people watch films on television or video but still enjoy going out to the cinema.

1930s

Going to the talking pictures or 'talkies' was a very popular pastime. People loved watching their favourite movie stars in glamorous films. Short news films were shown, too.

1960s

Fewer people went out to see films. They watched television at home instead. Lots of cinemas were closed down or turned into Bingo halls.

Now

New, exciting films have made going to the cinema popular once again. Multi-screen cinemas have lots of little cinemas under one roof. There is usually a film to suit everyone.

Glossary

barrow   a small cart which can be pushed around by hand

carriages   wheeled vehicles that people travelled in, usually pulled by horses

customers   people who buy things from shops or markets

dairies   companies that sell milk and food made from milk, such as cheese, butter and cream

household goods   things which are used in the home; dusters, cleaners, dishcloths, clothes pegs or bin bags are just a few examples

patients   people who are sick and who go to hospital to be looked after

Books
to read

History From Objects series by Karen Bryant-Mole (Wayland 1994)

History From Photographs series by Kath Cox and Pat Hughes (Wayland 1995-6)

How We Used to Live 1954-1970 by Freda Kelsall (A&C Black 1987)

Looking Back series (Wayland 1991)

Acknowledgements

The Publishers would like to thank the following for allowing their pictures to be used in this book: Beamish, The North of England Open Air Museum 4 & cover, 5 (left), 6, 7 (left & cover), 8, 9 (left), 10, 11, 12, 13 (left), 14, 15 (left), 16, 17 (left), 18 (both), 19 (left), 20, 21 (left), 22 (both), 23 (left), 24, 25 (left), 26 (both), 27 (left); Eye Ubiquitous 5 (right, Paul Seheult), 7 (right, Paul Seheult), 9 (right & cover, Paul Thompson), 11 (right, Paul Seheult), 17 (right, Paul Thompson), 21 (right, David Cumming), 25 (right, L. Johnstone), 29 (right, Paul Seheult); Granada 29 (left); Kobal Collection 28; Zefa 27 (right); Zul Mukhida/Chapel Studios 13 (right), 15 (right), 19 (right), 23 (right).

They would also like to thank the staff of Worthing Library.

Index